"In the

Roman

roads

but the...

The internet is our Roman road today. ... *used for good, but Christians have the opportunity to have a powerful missional presence in the digital world.* Digital Dominion *is an incredible roadmap to tell us how believers should travel these roads today."*

Thom S. Rainer, Founder and CEO, Church Answers; Author of *The Post-Quarantine Church*

"Digital discipleship is an emerging area of urgent focus in pastoral ministry. How do we become faithful disciples of Jesus in such an over-stimulated, often-unwise digital age? How can we make sure technology isn't using us *more than we're using it? Jeff Mingee's book is an excellent, practical engagement with these timely questions. Those in ministry or training for ministry would benefit greatly from applying the book's wisdom in their lives and ministry spheres. We need to be asking these questions and having these conversations!"*

Brett McCracken, Senior Editor, The Gospel Coalition; Author of *The Wisdom Pyramid: Feeding Your Soul in a Post-Truth World*

"Digital devices, like all devices, have the power to bless or curse, to build up or tear down. Without wisdom from above and the moral steel to act on that wisdom, we will be cursed and possibly destroyed by the plethora of digital devices at our fingertips. Digital Dominion *is both timely and desperately needed in our day. It is grounded in biblical and theological truth. It is also practical and sensible. Read it with much profit and then go and put what you have learned into practice."*

Daniel L. Akin, President, Southeastern Baptist Theological Seminary

"Christians today live in the digital age, with its perils and promise. This requires an awareness of and discipleship toward healthy habits of engagement with our devices and with the interconnectedness of the world. Digital Dominion *is a helpful guide to steer us away from two extremes: either total disengagement or total immersion. This issue of digital stewardship is one of the most important discipleship issues of our time. And this book is a must-read for anyone, from pastor to parent to plumber, who wishes to honor Christ well with their online lives."*

Daniel Darling, Director, Land Center for Cultural Engagement at Southwestern Baptist Theological Seminary; Bestselling author of several books including *The Dignity Revolution, The Characters of Christmas,* and *A Way with Words: Using Our Online Conversations for Good*

Digital Dominion

Digital Dominion

FIVE QUESTIONS CHRISTIANS SHOULD ASK TO TAKE CONTROL OF THEIR DIGITAL DEVICES

JEFF MINGEE

First published in Great Britain in 2022

British Library Cataloguing in Publication Data

A record for this book is available from the British Library

ISBN: 978-1-914966-44-6

Designed and typeset by Pete Barnsley (CreativeHoot.com)

Printed in Denmark by Nørhaven

10Publishing, a division of 10ofthose.com
Unit C, Tomlinson Road, Leyland, PR25 2DY, England

Email: info@10ofthose.com
Website: www.10ofthose.com

1 3 5 7 10 8 6 4 2

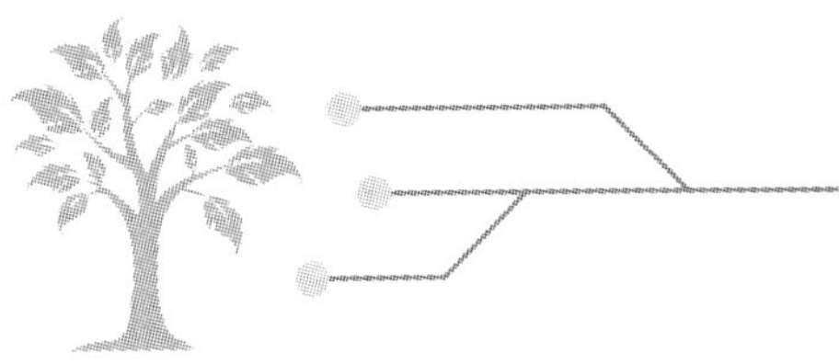

Contents

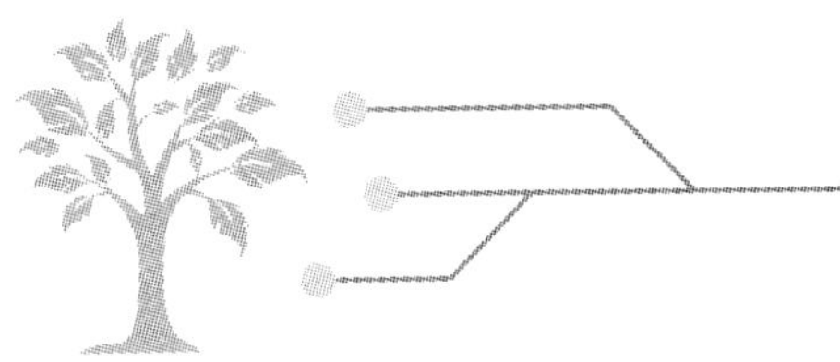

Introduction

Part of responsible, wise, faithful use of tools is analyzing the ways that certain tools shape us to see the world in certain ways, and then to ask whether those ways are consistent with the life of a disciple of Christ.

Jacob Shatzer[1]

The questions you ask determine the answers you get. In this book, we're going to ask five questions about our digital devices and our digital habits. Along the way, we will uncover sobering statistics about our practices as well as consider

1 Jacob Shatzer, *Transhumanism and the Image of God: Today's Technology and the Future of Christian Discipleship* (Downers Grove: Intervarsity, 2019), p. 7.

new, and more life-giving, habits. We'll move from being unintentional to being purposeful.

Wise Christians are running the wrong way with digital devices. Like children with scissors, some sprint without care and others freeze in fear. Dread tells us never to move with scissors. Wisdom teaches us *how* to move with them.

We need to know *how* to use our digital devices.

While I certainly understand, and sometimes applaud, a reasoned retreat or season of disconnecting from the digital world, I also feel a sense of remorse when wise Christians check out of the digital sphere. It's one less light in a very dark space. One less missionary on a very lost field. We need their voice not their vacancy.

I get the misgivings Christians have. I too am weary of the digital world. Yet the answer to our weariness is not abandonment, but dominion.

Dominion will help us control our devices instead of being controlled by our devices. Our digital world influences us with each notification, app, and upgrade. We are swimming in a digital culture which calls for digital wisdom. And like our inflatable floaties, wisdom is only good if we use it. We need control in our digital lives. That's what dominion is: wisdom applied.

Christians apply biblical wisdom to their digital practices. Biblical wisdom is a lamp unto our digital feet and a light unto our digital path.[2] This light exposes the realities of our digital habits. It provides wisdom for those willing to apply it.

Missionary Lesslie Newbigin returned to England after serving for decades on a foreign mission field. Reflecting on his homeland after an extended time away, Newbigin observed, "It is only as the fruit of sustained exposure to the Bible that one begins to see familiar things in a new light."[3] Our digital devices are now familiar things. They require sustained exposure to the Bible. Failing to shine the light of Scripture on our digital devices will have dramatic consequences. As our digital devices shape us, we need wisdom to exercise dominion over them.

---

2 This idea was originally presented by Bruce Ashford, Lecture for DMin 8504, Southeastern Baptist Theological Seminary (October 2018), paraphrasing Psalm 119:105.

3 Lesslie Newbigin, *Foolishness to the Greeks: The Gospel and Western Culture* (Grand Rapids: Eerdmans, 1986), p. 8.

My aim is to equip you to take control of your digital devices. Throughout the book, I will refer to technology. While technology includes a variety of subcategories, we will focus on digital devices. God intends for you to take control—to exercise dominion—over your digital devices.

There is little doubt that you are digitally engaged. Take a look around. How many digital devices are within eyesight in this moment, or when you're sitting in your living room? Next time you're at a stoplight, notice how many people are looking at their phones. When you're grabbing coffee with your friend, notice whether or not your phones are on the table. Are they face up? How many times are you distracted from your friend by a notification?

Americans spend an average of five and a half hours a day with digital media, more than half of that time on mobile devices, according to the research firm eMarketer. Among some groups, the numbers range much higher. In one recent survey, female students at Baylor University reported using their cell phones an average of ten hours a day. Three quarters of eighteen-to-twenty-year-olds say that they reach for

> *their phones immediately upon waking up in the morning. Once out of bed, we check our phones 221 times a day—an average of every 4.3 minutes—according to a UK study. This number actually may be too low, since people tend to underestimate their own mobile usage. In a 2015 Gallup survey, 61 percent of people said they checked their phones less frequently than others they knew.*[4]

This is our world. And this is us.

Perhaps I should clarify. This is not only "us." More precisely, "this is me." I'm not writing this book for you, but for myself. I'm not only disheartened and concerned over your digital habits. I'm far more concerned and far more disheartened over my own. Too often I find myself mindlessly scrolling while loved ones sit nearby. Too often I find myself with a day that reflects more time on social media than in communion with God. I think about who I am becoming, and I don't always like the answer. I belong to Jesus and I have so much joy to

---

4 Jacob Weisberg, "We Are Hopelessly Hooked," *The New York Review of Books* (February 25, 2016); https://www.nybooks.com/issues/2016/02/25/

discover in a life lived in obedience to him. I do not want to waste it staring at a screen that fits into the palm of my hands.

As I have already mentioned, we will—after an introductory chapter—explore five questions aimed at helping you regain control of your digital devices. In chapter one, we will discover how God's command to exercise dominion applies to our digital devices. In chapter two, we ask, "Am I in control?" In chapter three, we explore the influence of our devices and habits through the question: "How is this shaping me?" In chapter four, we consider God's aim for humanity and whether or not our devices serve that aim as we ask, "Does this help me flourish?" In chapter five, we shine the light of biblical wisdom on our digital habits with the question: "Can I discern wisdom and folly?" Finally, in chapter six, we move from being passive recipients to purposeful users for Christ's glory: "Am I being missional?"

Our dependence on digital technology is not going anywhere anytime soon. Arguably, it will increase. As people responded to the Covid-19 pandemic in 2020, they shifted even more of their lives online. After telling students that they needed to detox from screen time, schools moved to digital learning and required students to spend untold hours in front of their devices. Employees moved to remote working. Churches shifted to streaming their services. The cause of social justice pulled advocates and those interested even further into their digital devices as they watched videos, read articles, and engaged in digital debates. These factors led Collin Hansen to recognize the digital dilemma as one of his top ten theology stories in 2020.[5]

For many Christians, failing to exercise digital dominion has gone hand in hand with neglecting our spiritual health. New apps and episodes fill our hearts more than new mercies. By regaining control we both reorient our hearts to Christ and repurpose our digital devices to make much of Christ.

My hope is that we can shine the light of the gospel onto our digital habits. Blogger Tim Challies explains, "Media ecologists like to remind us that our technologies are extensions of ourselves and our abilities, so that the hammer is an extension of the arm and the

---

5 https://www.thegospelcoalition.org/article/my-top-10-theology-stories-of-2020/

bicycle is an extension of the feet."[6] Our digital devices are extensions of our hands and, further still, our hearts. The gospel explains that our hearts, our very selves, are made in the image of a holy God who is our Creator. In his kindness, he has given us good rules by which to live and enjoy his kingship. Since the time of Adam and Eve, however, we have turned our hearts in other directions, all in disobedience to him. As a result of this rebellion, we have lost the original enjoyment of our heavenly Father. We are now enemies of the God who made us and are bent on living out this enmity in every arena of our lives. And so we would remain but for Jesus. Sent by God, Christ lived the obedient life that we failed to live. Commissioned by God, Christ died on the cross—bearing the punishment that each of us rightly deserved as God's enemies. On the cross, God poured his righteous wrath on his Son in our place. Buried, Jesus proved his authority over sin and death through his resurrection three days later. And God now reconciles us to himself by faith in this crucified and risen King.

---

6 Tim Challies, "Advanced Technologies and Basic Christianity;" https://www.challies.com/articles/advanced-technologies-and-basic-christianity/ (accessed February 6, 2019).

For those of us who are in Christ, this gospel changes everything. At a basic level, it changes ownership. We are no longer our own. We have been bought with a price. Therefore, we are to glorify God in our bodies and with every extension of those bodies, including our digital devices.

Dominion

And God blessed them. And God said to them, "Be fruitful and multiply and fill the earth and subdue it, and have dominion. . . ."

Gen. 1:28

God desires for his people to live purposefully in both their living rooms and the digital world. He has sent you into the world to display his goodness and glory not accidentally, but on purpose. God has no wandering arrows. You are meant to exercise digital dominion.

God Sets the Stage for Digital Dominion

Genesis 1 displays God's unrivaled authority in creation. He needs no substance to work with as, out of nothing, he creates. With the power of his voice alone, God speaks the world into existence. And, before you start to feel a sense of similar power, no, using voice activation to turn on the bathroom light does not compare. God stands alone as Creator over his creation.

We find our devices selling us the enticing lie that we are gods in our own right; that we have original creative power. Like Eve, we gladly buy the lie. But the opening chapters of Genesis remind us that there is only one God and it is not us.

First, God creates light. Second, he creates the heavens. Third, the earth and seas. God is setting the stage. Fourth, he brings up vegetation from the created earth. Fifth, God places the stars, each of which he knows by name. Sixth, God fills the seas and the earth with living creatures. And he did it without David Attenborough of *Planet Earth* narrating in the background. Now, the earth pulses with life. God wrote and directed the opening act. He set the stage for the pinnacle moment of creation.

The author of Genesis records, "Then God said, 'Let us make man in our image, after our likeness. And let them have dominion over the fish of the sea and over the birds of the heavens and over the livestock and over all the earth and over every creeping thing that creeps on the earth'" (Gen. 1:26). This crowning act of creation stands unique from all the others.

After recording this creative act of God, the author explains, "So God created man in his own image, in the image of God he created him; male and female he created them" (Gen. 1:27). Humans, not animals, are notably made in the image of God. God gave humans, not plants, the command to exercise dominion. Humanity holds a privileged place among the rest of creation. Humans are set in a position of submission as they are made "in the image of God" and yet in a position of authority as they are given dominion over creation. God created you to exercise dominion in submission to his authority, and I don't think he meant you building your island in an online game.

Image and Authority

Humans are created in the image of God. While Christians can disagree over what exactly this means, they cannot disagree that it is a fact. God created every human being in his image. Additionally, God gave humanity dominion over the earth. Human beings bear both image and authority.

Before we gloss over this too quickly, let's pause and ask a simple question: Do you realize every person is created in the image of God? The image of God is not reserved for people that vote like us or dress like us or believe like us. The image of God is a universal reality. This impacts how we treat people, whether in the womb or crossing a border, whether we interact with them face to face or through a screen.

Among creation, God uniquely created humanity in his image. This gives humanity more value than other parts of creation—whether that is a Kapok tree God made in the Amazon jungle, or a cell phone, made by humans from God's resources, in the display window of an Apple store. Humans hold intrinsic value that trees, and devices, do not. Humans are always more important than a digital device.

After embracing this divine image that humanity bears, can you also appreciate the authority that humanity has been given? It is no small thing to be human. God himself has commanded humanity to subdue the earth and have dominion over the created world. He did not give this authority to dirt or birds or the wind, but to humanity. And humanity exercises this authority as an act of faithful stewardship—a theme we will discuss later.

Now, bad theologians have turned these opening biblical texts into tortured prisoners of war, twisting them until they say what their captors want to hear. These texts have been misapplied to justify men dominating women and humans exploiting creation. But we should not allow their bad applications to get in the way of our good understanding. Humanity has been placed as stewards of God's good world. K.A. Mathews explains, "Human life then bears this responsibility under God and is held accountable for the world God has created for humanity to govern, for 'the earth he has given to ... man'

(Ps. 115:16)."[7] God has created us to faithfully exercise dominion over creation. For this, and to him, we will one day give an account.

Dominion Defined

God placed Adam and Eve in the garden and invested authority and responsibility in them. He did not give them unlimited authority. He gave them a job to fulfill: "And God blessed them. And God said to them, 'Be fruitful and multiply and fill the earth and subdue it, and have dominion over the fish of the sea and over the birds of the heavens and over every living thing that moves on the earth'" (Gen. 1:28). This dominion deserves definition.

Biblical dominion carries connotations of authority, stewardship, creation, and cultivation. For the purposes of this book, and our application of dominion to the digital realm, we will define dominion as, "creating out of that which God has created and stewarding what has been created." We exercise dominion by creating out of the raw materials which God has created and

---

7 K.A. Mathews, *Genesis 1–11:26*, The New American Commentary, vol. 1A (Nashville: Broadman & Holman Publishers, 1996), p. 175.

by stewarding those creations for God's glory and our good.

Andy Crouch explains,

> *The author [of Genesis 1] clearly intends us to grasp the extent of human beings' responsibility—they are made to rule not just a few easily domesticated animals like cattle, chickens and goldfish, but the whole panoply of the animal kingdom. It's extraordinary that a biblical author who had seen neither airplanes nor submarines, and for whom boats were small and rudimentary affairs, could anticipate humankind being able to "rule" over fish and birds in any meaningful way. Either the author's conception of rule and dominion is much less about the naked exertion of power than we might imagine, or this text anticipates millennia of cultural developments that would eventually bring us to the point where we truly have the power to shape the destiny of most species on the planet.*[8]

---

8 Andy Crouch, *Culture Making: Recovering Our Creative Calling* (Downers Grove: Intervarsity, 2008), pp. 102–103.

Dominion in Genesis 1 foreshadows our dominion in a digital age. Crouch explains that as God cultivated the earth, he was, "paying attention to what already exists and what will be the most fruitful and beautiful use of it; most of all, what will most contribute to the flourishing of the human beings he is about to create."[9] Imagine if the creators of technology yet to be released were driven by such a desire!

But let's get back to us. We do not exercise dominion by blindly buying the newest cell phone or downloading every app promoted by pop-up ads. We exercise digital dominion by carefully creating devices, by intentionally purchasing and obtaining devices (saying, "No, I will not purchase that device" may itself be an act of dominion), and by maintaining wise practices as we use these devices.

Dominion throughout the Bible

Genesis 1 records the first command to exercise dominion. God said to Adam and Eve, "have dominion" (Gen. 1:28). Like a seed growing into a tree with multiple branches, the command

---

9 Crouch, *Culture Making*, p. 108.

grows into a scriptural theme with multiple expressions. Throughout the Old Testament narratives, we read of God's people exercising dominion—sometimes well. They exercised dominion over the created world as they constructed buildings and designed cities. As early as Genesis 4 we read of Cain developing a city (Gen. 4:17). The tower of Babel (Gen. 11) proves that this development was not always done out of obedience to God. The people of God exercised dominion as they subdued God's enemies in obedience to his direction.

In the wisdom literature, God's people find practical help as they exercise dominion over time (Ecc. 3:1–8), energy (Prov. 20:29), fear (Prov. 22:19), temptation (Prov. 1:10), and money (Prov. 17:16 – it applies to digital currency, too!). The entire category of wisdom literature in Scripture could be summarized as how to exercise godly dominion over all of life. The prophets echo the call to dominion as they contrast the evil rule of unbelieving nations against the kind and righteous rule of God. As God's people heard the word of the prophets and the sweet reminder of God's reign, they were reminded of their responsibility to steward life well as they waited for God to restore creation under his dominion.

The theme of exercising dominion continues in the New Testament. The gospel writers present Jesus as exercising dominion out of obedience to God. Jesus explains, "Truly, truly, I say to you, the Son can do nothing of his own accord, but only what he sees the Father doing. For whatever the Father does, that the Son does likewise" (John 5:19). Jesus displays his authority as he teaches (Mark 1:21–22). He exorcises demons, proving his dominion over the supernatural (Mark 1:23–26). Through miracles such as the calming of the storm, Jesus shows his dominion over the natural world (Matt. 8:23–27). He displays his authority as he exercises control over disease through the miracles of healing (Mark 5). Jesus even exerts dominion over death (Mark 16:6).

As Jesus concludes his earthly ministry, he states,

> *All authority in heaven and on earth has been given to me. Go therefore and make disciples of all nations, baptizing them in the name of the Father and of the Son and of the Holy*

> *Spirit, teaching them to observe all that I have commanded you. And behold, I am with you always, to the end of the age" (Matt. 28:18–20).*

Jesus thus charges the disciples—and the church—to continue his work. In doing so, he reiterates the cultural mandate given to Adam and Eve in Genesis 1. G.K. Beale explains, "The cultural mandate (in Genesis 1) is the first Great Commission (which is clarified in Matthew 28)."[10] So, the church is to live and act in a way that exalts the authority of Jesus. And we are to steward our lives, our bodies, our time, and our digital devices to make Christ known.

A Call to Digital Dominion

I hope you're convinced that you have a job to do. If you're a Christian, you should recognize through Scripture that God has given you a good command and called you to exercise dominion over the created world. It's a responsibility you cannot ignore.

---

10 https://www.thegospelcoalition.org/article/what-is-the-relationship-between-the-cultural-mandate-and-the-great-commission/

Every arena of life requires dominion, including the digital one. That phone within arm's reach right now (yep, I've got you figured out already!)—how quickly could it demand your full attention? What would it take? A buzz? A ding? What if the screen lit up to show an incoming message? Or maybe just a small blinking light would be enough for you to stop what you're doing and obey. Wait a minute . . . who has dominion over who? Who is really in control?

Christian, Jesus has commissioned you to be his witness to the ends of the earth . . . and the digital world (Acts 1:8). How will you steward this life for that task? Paul commands us, "So, whether you eat or drink, or whatever you do, do all to the glory of God" (1 Cor. 10:31). We know our task: to live in a way that promotes the glory of God in Christ and the good of all people. We know we will give an account. Will we hear, "Well done, good and faithful servant?" (Matt. 25:23)? Will we take control, and exercise dominion, of our digital world?

Discussion Questions

Here—and at the end of each chapter—are some questions to prompt your own further thinking or for group discussion with others:

1. How many digital devices are within your eyesight right now?
2. We are made in the image of God (*imago dei*) and have been given authority to exercise dominion. How do these doctrines impact your use of digital devices?
3. In what ways do you see people failing to honor the image of God in others through digital devices?
4. In what ways do you fail to obey the command to have dominion with your digital devices?
5. Jeff writes, "We do not exercise dominion by blindly buying the newest phone or downloading every app promoted by pop-up ads. We exercise

digital dominion by carefully creating devices, by intentionally purchasing and obtaining devices (saying, 'No, I will not purchase that device' may itself be an act of dominion), and by maintaining wise practices as we use these devices." How else can we exercise digital dominion?

Am I in Control?

If we're serious about developing self-control we need to be aware of how new technologies tax our restraint.

Drew Dyck[11]

Am I in control? That's the first question we should ask. Are we controlling our devices or have they begun to control us? Digital devices open up a world of possibilities. We can connect with distanced loved ones. We can transfer

11 Drew Dyck, *Your Future Self Will Thank You: Secrets to Self-Control from the Bible and Brain Science* (Chicago: Moody, 2019), p. 166.

money at the touch of a button. We can navigate remote terrain.

At the same time, digital devices can lure us into addiction. Perhaps you feel the pang of guilt over spending too much time on your digital devices. Parents see their children become short-tempered after uninterrupted hours in front of a screen (or so I've heard). A spouse looks up from their phone only to notice that their loved one left the room . . . but who knows when? (Again, I'm clearly not writing from personal experience.)

The biblical authors use the language of "dominion" to explain humanity's God-given authority over creation. We were made to exercise dominion (Gen. 1:28). We were made, under the authority of God, to exercise control. But when it comes to our digital devices, we are tempted to forego mindful dominion and instead enter in with mindless consumption. So, who is controlling who?

Out-of-Control Saints Don't Glorify God

Against the backdrop of God creating humanity to exercise dominion, consider the man who misses his son score the winning goal because he is distracted by the vibrating phone in his pocket. Or the young employee who browses social media but with the mouse cursor hovering over the "x," ready to close it should her boss walk by. Or the student who ignores his body's cry for sleep and instead strains his tired eyes to scroll for a few more images. They are not in control.

Paul warned of those who weren't in control. He described one controlling factor of enemies of the cross as, "their god is their belly" (Phil. 3:19). Idolatrous passions or earthly concerns governed them. They were out of control. In contrast, Paul exemplified the importance of control in the Christian life (1 Cor. 9:27).

Paul knew that out-of-control saints don't glorify God. We are to exercise control because we believe that God deserves our active obedience and not merely our accidental praise. Yes, he will ultimately be glorified even if we rebel against him. But he is worthy of our lives—even our digital lives.

God created you to have control over creation. He did not intend for you to be controlled by your device. Rather, he intended you to use it for his good purposes. When it comes to the digital world, many of us are out of control, but what if we exercised digital control in obedience to the greatest and second commandment? What if you took control of your devices as an act of love toward God and love toward your neighbor?

Digital Control and Love of God

Jesus said the greatest commandment was to "love the Lord your God with all your heart and with all your soul and with all your mind" (Matt. 22:37). If you want to process how to steward your digital devices in obedience to Jesus, this is a pretty good place to start. Take control of your digital devices because you love God.

The Christian life requires control. Without it, we're drifting; and no one drifts in the right direction.

We practice digital control for the glory of Christ. Our aim is that through us others might see how great Christ is. But that requires control.

We exercise dominion ultimately to fill the earth with image-bearers and to glorify God. David Mathis explains, "Christian self-control is not finally about bringing our bodily passions under our own control, but under the control of

Christ by the power of his Spirit."[12] We're not seeking control over our digital devices merely for productivity or for our own fame. We're seeking control over them to make much of Christ, a task which we will turn our attention to more directly in a later chapter. Christian men and women are gladly under the rule and reign of Jesus. His commands are never burdensome (1 John 5:3). Obedience to Jesus brings joy, even in the digital world.

In Galatians 5, the apostle Paul lists evidences of the Holy Spirit's work in our lives. Among this list he includes "self-control" (Gal 5:23). Self-control is not mere effort. Christians, as we pursue self-control in our digital habits, recognize that such a fruit is a result of the Holy Spirit's work in our lives. This impacts both how we understand self-control and the means we use to pursue it.

In addition to Paul's description of self-control as a fruit of the Holy Spirit, he also directly ties it to our salvation. In explaining the gospel of Jesus Christ to Felix and his wife Drusilla, Paul

---

12 David Mathis, "Self-Control and the Power of Christ;" https://www.desiringgod.org/articles/self-control-and-the-power-of-christ

thought it necessary to reason about self-control (Acts 24:24–25). Self-control is an essential part of us working out our own salvation. Like an athlete developing self-control in the pursuit of a win, Christians develop self-control in the pursuit of our ultimate salvation (1 Cor. 9:25). We cannot take our sanctification seriously while dismissing the need for self-control, not even in the digital world.

Digital Control and Love of Neighbor

What is your lack of digital control doing to those you love? Do your kids feel unheard? Does your spouse feel neglected? I know you really want to beat that next level, but is it worth the cost of these relationships?

If I want to love my wife well, I need to control myself. If I want to serve her by making her a smoothie before she heads to school with the kids, I need enough control to put my phone down. If I want to love my son by playing football or a board game with him, I must have the self-discipline to close the app or computer. Our failure to develop self-control stifles our love for others. Our digital devices are not helping.

We've all felt the sting of neglect as someone chose to pay attention to a device instead of us. Perhaps they didn't mean to hurt us. But we asked the same question multiple times and got no response. We tried to move closer to them, but were unable to get their attention. We sought intimacy, but only got isolation.

May it not be so with you. Develop control as an act of love toward others. Exercise digital dominion as a display of affection toward those you cherish. Don't hand over control of your life to a digital device. Take control and love others well.

Exercising Digital Dominion

So, how are you doing in the digital domain? The statistics suggest that you're probably not doing very well; that you're not in control. When your phone buzzes, you'll look. In fact, you'll probably feel a phantom buzz if it's been in your pocket for too long. Nothing has happened. No notifications have gone off. But the mere thought that they might causes you to imagine that they have. You are not in control.

Perhaps you're wondering if control is even possible. Tony Reinke asks, "So what sort of freaks of self-control must we become to resist the well-engineered marshmallows of distraction? Freaks who believe in 2 Corinthians 4:18, who 'look not to the things that are seen but to the things that are unseen. For the things that are seen are transient, but the things that are unseen are eternal.'"[13] You can't exercise dominion in the digital world until you exercise self-control in your daily life.

The good news is that self-control is not a product of self-effort; it's a fruit of the Spirit of God at work in you (Gal. 5:22–23). God not only expects you to exercise dominion and control; he empowers you for the work.

Better control is not necessarily to use our devices less, but to use them with greater wisdom. We want to use our devices for human flourishing and for the advancement of the gospel. We want to take better control of our devices not so that we can look down on less-disciplined users with pride, but so that we can—without distraction—look up to Christ with awe.

---

13 Tony Reinke, *12 Ways Your Phone Is Changing You* (Wheaton: Crossway, 2017), p. 89.

God has made humanity in his image and entrusted to them the task of the cultural mandate. We are to exercise dominion in the digital world! We are to be not only the creators of technology, but stewards of it as well. Both the privilege and the responsibility call for intentionality. Both carry massive implications for our digital engagement. What push notifications should we allow to interrupt us? Should data tracking and cell-phone tracing be encouraged or outlawed in a global pandemic? If technological advances can flirt with creating life, should they be pursued? Technology allows me to send a picture of my son skateboarding to his aunt in another city. But the same technology can be used to fuel the sex-slave trade by sending pictures of young women. If we fail to take control, the dangers are paramount.

In contrast, if we do take control, we can leverage our devices for great gain! There are apps that can help you memorize Scripture and prompt you to pray. Technology can connect you with global missionaries. One summer afternoon I sat on my back porch in Virginia and had a conversation with one of our missionaries in Southeast Asia. You can watch an evangelistic video with that family member who lives in another part of the world and then discuss it over a video chat. You can find soul-strengthening fellowship with that friend who just moved out of state. Oh, God offers us great blessings to enjoy through our digital devices . . . if we take control.

Discussion Questions

1. On a scale of 1 to 10 (1 being not at all in control and 10 being totally in control), where would you place yourself right now? If you're reading this book with friends, ask them where they would place you.

2. Imagine you completely lost control of your digital devices and digital habits. List five ways that would harm yourself and the people you care about.

3. How might developing better digital control help you to love God more? How might developing better digital control help you to love others more?

4. Who is one person you could use your digital device to bless with an encouraging call or message? Make that call or send that message now.
5. What is one way you can exercise control over your digital devices today?

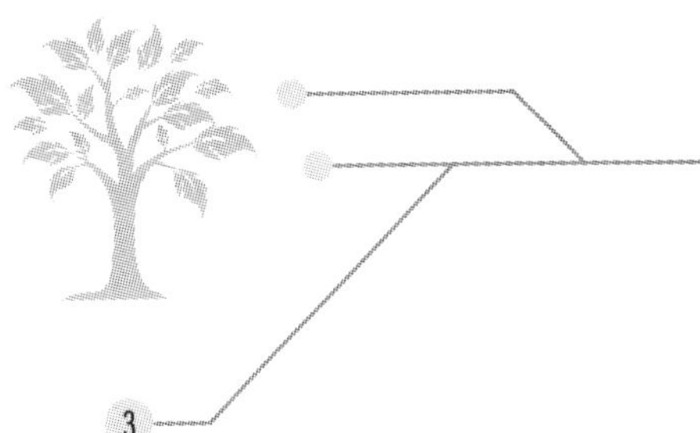

How Is This Shaping Me?

We make our technologies, and they, in turn, shape us.

Sherry Turkle[14]

Do you check your phone first thing when you wake up? How do you use it throughout your day? Where do you put your devices when you sleep? Like the nightly bowl of ice cream, some digital

14 Sherry Turkle, *Alone Together: Why We Expect More from Technology and Less from Each Other* (New York: Basic Books, 2011), p. 19.

habits are less than healthy. But can you see the cumulative effect of such unhealthy practices?

Theologian James K.A. Smith contends that our habits, which he calls "liturgies," shape us. Opening email before you say "hello" to your spouse is not just a bad habit; it's a character-producing habit. Smith explains, "Liturgies [another word for patterns or regular practices]—whether 'sacred' or 'secular'—shape and constitute our identities by forming our most fundamental desires and our most basic attunement to the world. In short, liturgies make us certain kinds of people."[15] Patterns of life, both intentional and unplanned, not only fill our calendars; they form our character. How are your devices shaping you?

Shaped by Something into Something

So, what happens when digital devices invade and even determine those habits? If our habits shape us, and if our habits are increasingly governed by the digital world, what kind of people are we becoming? Sherry Turkle, founder and director

---

15 James K.A. Smith, *Desiring the Kingdom: Worship, Worldview, and Cultural Formation* (Grand Rapids: Baker Academic, 2009), p. 25.

of the MIT Initiative on Technology and Self, observes, "We make our technologies, and they, in turn, shape us."[16] What is the cumulative effect of these digital liturgies and habits? Technology influences both individuals and communities.

Community businesses and non-profits strategically engage digital platforms and offer digital connectivity to remain relevant. Even local parks and recreation centers provide free Wi-Fi connections. But does that enable the young mother to video chat with her sister who lives internationally, showing her how little Johnny can go down the slide by himself? Or does it pull that young mother's attention into her palm while little Johnny plays out of sight? Community and individual connectivity shape our world and shape us. We are becoming a certain type of person as we pursue this digital vision of the good life.

A Daily Digital Liturgy

I would like to invite you to observe a day in the life of the stereotypical digital worshipper. At a precise and predetermined time, our subject

16 Turkle, *Alone Together*, p. 19.

is hijacked from rest with the repeated and increasingly loudening buzzes from her phone, carefully positioned within reach of her bed. She reaches from under the covers and silences the alarm with a quick swipe of her thumb. She has been digitally aroused (which may take on a whole different meaning later in the day, given statistics).

A moment later, she stretches the power cord as far as allowed—further than the frayed cable and exposed wires recommend. She has stretched and twisted that cord one too many times. Her eyes adjust to the glowing screen. She is slowly coming to life with the nurturing help of her device. Having silenced the alarm, she checks social media to see what others have considered worth informing the digital world about while she was asleep. Her eyes scan headlines that report increasing global crises, accompanied by the furious comments of her friends, family, and coworkers—quickening her heartbeat before she's even thought about exercise. With another click she has left her social circle for email and begins to browse through her collected mailbox. She sorts between daily real-estate updates in her desired neighborhood (a reminder of what she does not have), promotions for local events (fueling her fear of missing out), and work-related updates (stirring anxiety and frustration for the day ahead). The mind that was sound asleep minutes ago is now swimming with a flurry of information.

As she gets out of bed and prepares for the day, her phone is never far from her. She uses it to check the weather forecast. She checks her schedule for the day. She responds to text messages and sends some of her own in hope of making plans for later. Notable events pop up on the screen from time to time and fill the air with chimes of notification, beckoning her back to the phone.

When she gets in the car to go to work, she uses the phone to listen to music and to direct her along the most time-efficient route, with boy-band-voiced directions warning her of hazards reported ahead. At work, she is plugged in to her computer yet keeps her phone nearby. In fact, every few minutes she checks it just to see if she missed anything. During the morning work routine, she connects via text message with her friend for lunch plans. She makes sure to set an alarm so she won't forget. At lunch, she holds her phone up to the register to pay, trading no niceties with the person behind the counter. While the friends eat, their conversation is driven by who posted what recently, and they both continue to check their phones throughout.

At the end of the workday, she heads home and uses her phone to look up the recipe for dinner as well as to time how long things need to cook. With her phone she watches TV and plays some games to pass a few hours. Of course, each event is interrupted a few times with a notification that something—either a funny meme from a friend or breaking news of a shooting—requires her attention. As she settles in for the night, she makes sure to plug her phone in so that it can recharge just as she does. They'll both need the energy to do it all again tomorrow.

Benefits and Dangers

As the above hypothetical scenario reminds us, the digital revolution provides benefits. It quickly connects us to more information and more people than any other time in history. Cross-country relocation no longer means the end of a relationship thanks to video-calling capabilities. We are a connected people. We wire money around the world. We are a people who expect easy access. Devices inform us of news in real time. We are informed people. The digital revolution enables us to accomplish more tasks in less time with less effort. We are always plugged-in.

We enjoy these benefits through digital practices and habits. Instead of watching a sunset, we snap a picture. Instead of having an in-person conversation, we send text messages. Is this good? The sunset turns from a moment of experience into a captured image that will outlast our memories and which can be shared, and even manipulated, via digital avenues. Family members can send the video of little Tommy scoring a goal in the soccer game to his aunt stationed overseas. Employees can format a conversation over the lunch table into a shared document that can be edited by parties at multiple times in multiple places.

People in both the secular and religious spheres enjoy the benefits of digital technology. Pastor John Piper explains, "For all the abuses and all the devastation of distraction, wasted hours, narcissistic self-promotion, and pornographic degradation, I see the computer and the smartphone as gifts of God—like papyrus and the codex and paper and the printing press and the organs of mass distribution."[17] These technological gifts open up a world of possibilities for users. William Powers, research scientist at the MIT Media Lab, reveals in his book *Hamlet's Blackberry*, "Two essential benefits digital connectedness confers: we can get everyday jobs done more easily *and* nurture our minds, hearts, and souls, all with a little gizmo that fits into our pockets."[18] The little gizmo produces gigantic benefits. Perhaps our devices are shaping us for the better.

Yet, the digital revolution contains dangers as well. Devices capture users' attention and erode face-to-face interaction. Recent surveys report that 89 percent of Americans say they interrupted their last social interaction to turn to their phones, and 82 percent say that the conversation suffered for it.[19] Tony Reinke explains,

---

17 Reinke, *12 Ways Your Phone Is Changing You*, p. 43.

18 William Powers, *Hamlet's Blackberry: A Practical Philosophy for Building a Good Life in the Digital Age* (New York: Harper Collins, 2010), p. 29.

19 Sherry Turkle, *The Second Self: Computers and the Human Spirit* (Cambridge, MA: MIT Press, 2005), p. 2.

> *The consequences are real. As digital distractions intrude into our lives at an unprecedented rate, behavioral scientists and psychologists offer statistical proof in study after study: the more addicted you become to your phone, the more prone you are to depression and anxiety, and the less able you are to concentrate at work and sleep at night. Digital distractions are no game.*[20]

These dangers and distractions carry personal and social consequences. We compare ourselves to photoshopped projections of other people who are comparing themselves to photoshopped projections of other people. Then we sink into depression when we don't measure up. The dangers threaten our relationships and more.

Netflix CEO and founder Reed Hastings reveals that Netflix's main competition is sleep: a competition that can't be good for humanity.[21] The "still watching?" prompt wants you to click yes, not to be well-rested. Our desire for

---

20 Reinke, *12 Ways Your Phone Is Changing You*, p. 43.

21 Rina Raphael, "Netflix CEO Reed Hastings: Sleep Is Our Competition," *Fast Company*; https://www.fastcompany.com/40491939/netflix-ceo-reed-hastings-sleep-is-our-competition/ (accessed November 1, 2018).

entertainment competes with our need for rest. The digital revolution bears some dangerous fruit. Perhaps our devices are shaping us for the worse.

The God Who Sanctifies

God created people with the potential to grow. He so ordered the physical world that we experience a process of growth as opposed to beginning as finished products. Puberty, with its squeaky voices and all, was his idea. God intends us to grow.

Jesus grew in wisdom and stature (Luke 2:52). Paul recalled his own growth from childhood to maturity (1 Cor. 13:11). Peter exhorted his readers to grow in grace (2 Pet. 3:18). Growth is good. But Paul also warned about being conformed to the world (Rom. 12:2). He warned Timothy of those who were "always learning and never able to arrive at a knowledge of the truth" (2 Tim. 3:7). Paul counseled the Corinthians, "Bad company ruins good morals" (1 Cor. 15:33).

You see, you are not just going through life. You are becoming something and someone—for better or for worse. As C.S. Lewis explains,

> *It is a serious thing to live in a society of possible gods and goddesses, to remember that the dullest and most uninteresting person you talk to may one day be a creature which, if you saw it now, you would be strongly tempted to worship, or else a horror and a corruption such as you now meet, if at all, only in a nightmare.... You have never talked to a mere mortal.*[22]

This means, of course, that neither are you a mere mortal. You, too, are on a trajectory that will never end but will lead to either a beautiful heaven or horrifying hell. And that digital device, without which you can't make it through a day, is pointing you in one of those two directions. That daily habit matters.

God revealed himself to Moses by saying, "I, the LORD, sanctify you" (Ex. 31:13). Sanctification is the work of God as he conforms us into the image of Christ. He is shaping you (Phil. 2:12–13). Shouldn't you reflect his sanctifying work in your digital habits?

---

22 C.S. Lewis, *The Weight of Glory* (originally published 1941; New York: Harper One, 2001), p. 45.

How Is This Shaping Me?

So, as you've considered your digital habits, how are they shaping you? What type of person are you becoming? And do you like what you see?

Consider your friend with bad digital habits. (Perhaps you're reading this book with them!) What are some of those bad habits? Do they constantly look at their phone while you are in the room? Do they seem to start sentences but never finish them because they get lost in scrolling? Do they start every conversation with, "Did you see what they posted?" It may be easier for you to identify how devices are shaping your friends than how they are shaping you.

Now, imagine that person kept those habits up for the next twelve months. Perhaps they kept those habits for the next five or even ten years. What effect do you think that would have on them? How would it impact their marriage? Would you want to be married to them? Then realize that your friends are asking the same questions about you.

You are being shaped by your digital habits. The question is: How? As you recognize the shaping effect of your digital habits, you're given the opportunity to curve the effect or redirect the trajectory. When you don't like the direction that your life—yes, even your digital life—seems to be heading, turn around or change direction!

An Unknown Future

We are being shaped, but into what? The future of the digital revolution remains unknown. Jacques Ellul warned, "Unpredictability is one of the general features of technological progress."[23] Turkle responds to this unpredictability: "We say 'yes' to new technology because we think we are getting something important from it.... But we need to get into new and more disciplined habits where we examine the assumption that we are getting something important from these new technologies."[24]

We are products of our digital age. We enjoy the benefits of faster productivity and increased accessibility to information. We suffer the consequences of distracted attention and anxiety-ridden minds. Our digital devices shape us for better or for worse. Recognizing the current

23 Reinke, *12 Ways Your Phone Is Changing You*, p. 18.

24 Turkle, *Alone Together*, p. xxii.

reality of our digital age, with all the benefits and dangers it holds, let us now consider the standard of God's vision for human flourishing.

Discussion Questions

1. Do your digital devices currently have a positive or negative impact on you? Are they shaping you for the better or for the worse?
2. As you read "A Daily Digital Liturgy," which moment most resonated with you? Was there a moment in which you thought, "Oh, that's me!"?
3. What are the benefits of your digital devices?
4. What are the dangers of your digital devices?
5. Think about God's sanctifying work in his people. How might he use digital devices in that work?

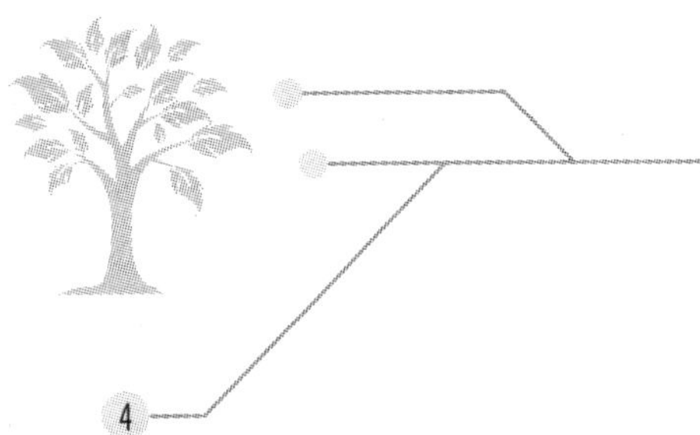

Does This Help Me Flourish?

What is the best use of my smartphone in the flourishing of my life?

Tony Reinke[25]

Just as every compass needle points in a direction relative to north—although I've had a few confused compasses—so every digital device points in a direction that envisions what humanity "should" be. In this chapter, I want

---

25 Reinke, *12 Ways Your Phone Is Changing You*, p. 20.

to compare the impact of our digital devices to God's intention for us. What kind of person is my phone making me? What kind of person does God intend me to be?

Do you think technology has been good for you? Has it helped you grow into a better person? We can measure the impact of our digital habits and liturgies by the standard of God's vision for human flourishing. Sherry Turkle from MIT warns, "So of every technology we must ask, does it serve our human purposes?—A question that causes us to reconsider what these purposes are."[26] Without an understanding of human purposes, digital participants may mindlessly accept everything labeled "good" as good indeed. We see nothing wrong with hours spent scrolling through posts, or watching endless programs via a streaming service. When the message pops up asking if we want to watch another episode, our instinctive response is, "Of course. Why shouldn't we?"

However, Neil Postman, writing amid the technological impact of television in the 1980s, cautions, "Only those who know nothing of the

---

26 Turkle, *Alone Together*, p. 19.

history of technology believe that a technology is entirely neutral."[27] Viewing another episode is another ingestion of a biased presentation, whether it's a news channel or an original series on some streaming service. Another social media app is another voice in the already crowded civic center of our phones. Not only is the content biased, but the tools themselves are bent in a certain direction. Postman again explains, "In every tool we create, an idea is embedded that goes beyond the function of the thing itself."[28] Every tool promotes a vision of the good life.

Every Tool a Guide

Every tool fuels the pursuit of a set of beliefs, a vision of human flourishing. We believe that human flourishing is the result of having unfiltered access to unfiltered content. So, we move to unlimited data plans. We believe the more we can accomplish faster, the better. So, the next device is always faster than the previous. We believe that self-expression is the way to self-

27 Neil Postman, *Entertaining Ourselves to Death: Public Discourse in the Age of Show Business* (New York: Penguin Books, 2006), p. 84.

28 Postman, *Entertaining Ourselves to Death*, p. 14.

discovery and self-fulfillment. So, each device provides more flexibility and improved features. These new abilities captivate us: "Seriously, you had me at 'slow-mo selfies.' How could I flourish without that?!"

These embedded ideas flow from an understanding of what it means for humans to thrive and flourish. But is it a good understanding? Is it correct?

Likewise, every group of people in every age builds a definition of human flourishing toward which they use those tools. Charles Taylor observes that "every person, and every society, lives with or by some conception(s) of what human flourishing is: what constitutes a fulfilled life? What makes life really worth living? What would we most admire people for?"[29] Someone's vision of what constitutes true human flourishing is driving our digital age, but whose?

God's vision of human flourishing did not govern the latest upgrades on your device. Therefore, be mindful. Tony Reinke warns

---

29 Charles Taylor, *A Secular Age* (Cambridge, MA: Belknap Press of Harvard University Press, 2007), p. 3, quoted in Dr David F. Ford, *God's Power and Human Flourishing: A Biblical Inquiry after Charles Taylor's* A Secular Age.

Christians, "Thoughtlessly adopting new technology is worldliness."[30] God's vision of human flourishing calls Christians out of thoughtless worldliness and into obedient godliness. We will not flourish while keeping God on the periphery.

Christians are to do everything for the glory of God (1 Cor. 10:31). This requires intentionality. We don't drift into God-glorifying behaviors; we intentionally seek them in obedience. Abraham Kuyper explains,

> *If everything that is, exists for the sake of God, then it follows that the whole creation must give glory to God. The sun, moon, and stars in the firmament, the birds of the air, the whole of nature around us, but, above all, man himself, who priest-like, must consecrate to God the whole of creation, and all life thriving in it. . . . Wherever man may stand, whatever he may do, to whatever he may apply his hand, in agriculture, in commerce, and in industry, or his mind, and in the world of art and science, he is, in whatsoever it may be,*

---

30 Reinke, *12 Ways Your Phone Is Changing You*, p. 37.

> *constantly standing before the face of God, he is employed in the service of God, he has strictly to obey his God, and above all, he has to aim at the glory of his God.*[31]

Kuyper exposes our digital engagement to our role as God's obedient children. We live before the face of God. We serve him. We do not get to check out of our obedience when we enter the digital realm. Digital life demands intentionality.

A Biblical Description of Human Flourishing

In the Christian worldview, flourishing is about realizing our potential as human beings made in the image of God. It is about becoming fruitful, creative, and relational human beings alongside the development of Christlike character.[32] Humans flourish best not when they express themselves most clearly, but when they bear the image of God most clearly. God's vision for

---

31 Abraham Kuyper, *Lectures on Calvinism* (Peabody, MA: Hendrickson, 2008), pp. 41–42.

32 Justin Taylor, "A Better Story: God, Sex, and Human Flourishing," The Gospel Coalition Blog (February 28, 2017); https://www.thegospelcoalition.org/blogs/justin-taylor/a-better-story-god-sex-and-human-flourishing/ (accessed November 15, 2018).

human flourishing is one in which we are aware of the shaping influence of our technologies and exercise dominion over them by remembering our Godward direction and holding to biblical wisdom in our usage. Additionally, God's vision includes us actively employing technology for his glory and humanity's good. How can we apply God's vision of flourishing to our digital world?

Bruce Ashford helps Christians discern God's good design and sin's destructive impact on our world. He offers a series of questions to ask: What is God's creational design for this realm of culture?[33] In Genesis 1:26, God reveals his intention in creating humans who would "have dominion" over animals and over all the earth—that is, dirt and air and molecules and electrons. God created humanity to exercise dominion in obedience to his good command to be fruitful and multiply, and to subdue and rule over the earth. Ashford continues, "The command to have dominion states directly that God wanted people to serve as loving managers of his good world."[34] God never intended for our world—or

---

33 Bruce Ashford, *Every Square Inch: An Introduction to Cultural Engagement for Christians* (Bellingham, WA: Lexham Press, 2015).

34 Ashford, *Every Square Inch*, p. 127.

our digital devices—to have dominion over us. God created humans to flourish by stewarding dominion, including over the digital realm, as they fill the earth with more image-bearers of their Creator God. This is human flourishing.

Yet, sin entered the world and we traded our God-centered stewardship for self-centered purposes. Ashford again guides us in our questions. We apply wisdom in discerning our sinful world by asking: How has this realm of culture been corrupted and misdirected by our sin and rebellion?

Yesteryear's technological advancements paved the way for our digital devices today. Advancement is a good thing. God's command to "cultivate" (Gen. 2:15) the creation implies a call to technological advancement. In cultivating the dirt into a garden, Adam and Eve would have designed tools—early technological tools—to fulfill the task. As the garden grew, the tools would have advanced as well. The structure of advancement is still good and for God's glory.

But the direction of advancement has been twisted from its Godward orientation. We now use technological advancement for our own fame and glory. We use it to distort a human life, or even to stop a living being from living altogether. We use technological advancement to bear false witness against our neighbor with a social media post. We obliterate our enemies either digitally in the court of public opinion or physically with technological weapons, both without fair trial. Sin erodes the Godward direction of our technological advances. This isn't hard to see: technological advancement is good, but humans have used it, even cultivated it, for evil. That is not what it means to flourish.

Humans living in a world twisted by sin must consider God's picture of human flourishing as the *telos*, or end, for which they strive. In contrast to Netflix's attempt to pull us from needed sleep, God's picture of human flourishing is the true vision of rest. We should work to keep this vision continually in mind.

God's people are a remembering people. With a device in our hands that constantly screams the momentary importance of breaking news, we are called to remember the never-changing good news of Christ. Indeed, if we want to flourish, this never-changing news ought to hold more governing influence over us than breaking news. The gospel is more real and true than the notification that just popped up on your phone. Remembering is part of the larger practice of applying godly wisdom and part of the pathway to flourishing.

God has given us the Scriptures for this very purpose of life and godliness. Biblical wisdom has much to say about our digital habits and liturgies. Solomon commands us to acknowledge God in all our ways (Prov. 3:6), which includes digital ways. He effectively warns us of the dangers of the digitally wicked whose iniquities "ensnare him. . . . He dies for lack of discipline, and because of his great folly he is led astray" (Prov. 5:22–23). Godly wisdom enables Christians to enjoy God's vision for human flourishing. Gordan Spykman clarifies, "Our calling is to bring the order *of* our life in God's world, whether in the pulpit or in politics, in our halls of learning or in our marketplaces, into conformity with God's good order *for* our life in his world."[35] God's people cast off godless

---

35 James Orr, *The Christian View of God and the World* (originally published 1893; reprinted Grand Rapids: Eerdmans, 1947), p. 4.

visions of flourishing and instead pursue God's vision of human flourishing.

Holiness in a Digital Age

Christians understand flourishing as holiness. Productivity and effectiveness and connectivity have their place in Christian flourishing, but at the heart of the matter is holiness. We cannot afford to assume this or to forget it.

Yet, we often neglect holiness in our discussions about digital devices and practices. The nineteenth-century pastor J.C. Ryle warned, "There has been of late years a lower standard of personal holiness among believers than there used to be in the days of our fathers. The whole result is that the Spirit is grieved and the matter calls for much humiliation and searching of heart."[36] Technological progress has not helped. Pastor Kevin DeYoung echoes Ryle's concern: "My fear is that as we rightly celebrate, and in some quarters rediscover, all that Christ has saved us from, we are giving little thought and making little effort concerning all

---

36 J.C. Ryle, *Holiness* (originally published 1877; reprinted Leyland: 10Publishing, 2017), p. 21.

that Christ has saved us to. Shouldn't those most passionate about the gospel and God's glory also be those most dedicated to the pursuit of godliness?"[37] Christian, are you dedicated to the pursuit of godliness in your life and with your digital devices?

Scripture celebrates and commands holiness in the life of a believer. The apostle Paul urges his readers to "know how to control his own body in holiness" (1 Thes. 4:4). We can safely assume he would have applied this to our scrolling fingers. He roots this expectation for holiness in the promises of God: "Since we have these promises, beloved, let us cleanse ourselves from every defilement of body and spirit, bringing holiness to completion in the fear of God" (2 Cor. 7:1). Additionally, he roots the expectation of holiness in our usefulness to God: "Therefore, if anyone cleanses himself from what is dishonorable, he will be a vessel for honorable use, set apart as holy, useful to the master of the house, ready for every good work" (2 Tim. 2:21). Paul holds an

37 Kevin DeYoung, *The Hole in Our Holiness: Filling the Gap between Gospel Passion and the Pursuit of Godliness* (Wheaton: Crossway, 2014). Adapted in https://www.crossway.org/articles/holiness-is-the-new-camping/

entry-level expectation for holiness among those who follow Jesus. So should we.

Peter also makes a clear call for holiness:

> *Therefore, preparing your minds for action, and being sober-minded, set your hope fully on the grace that will be brought to you at the revelation of Jesus Christ. As obedient children, do not be conformed to the passions of your former ignorance, but as he who called you is holy, you also be holy in all your conduct, since it is written, "You shall be holy, for I am holy" (1 Pet. 1:13–16).*

Your conversion ought to impact your internet searches and scrolling habits.

But what is holiness and how do we exhibit it in a digital world? Again, Ryle's voice rises above the rest: "Holiness is the habit of being of one mind with God, according as we find His mind described in Scripture. It is the habit of agreeing in God's judgment – hating what He hates – loving what He loves – and measuring everything in this world by the standard of His

Word."[38] Does "of one mind with God" describe your digital habits?

Kevin DeYoung explains,

> *Holiness is the sum of a million little things—the avoidance of little evils and little foibles, the setting aside of little bits of worldliness and little acts of compromise, the putting to death of little inconsistencies and little indiscretions, the attention to little duties and little dealings, the hard work of little self-denials and little self-restraints, the cultivation of little benevolences and little forbearances.*[39]

Be holy.

As with all things in the digital world, we need to beware of our inner Pharisee that cares for the outside of the cup without caring for the inside. Beware of creating a digital profile that looks holy instead of pursuing true holiness. As you consider whether or not your digital devices help you flourish, value holiness as the goal of your flourishing.

---

38 Ryle, *Holiness*, p. 56.

39 DeYoung, *The Hole in Our Holiness*, p. 145.

The Call for Technology's Proper Place

Andy Crouch, executive director of *Christianity Today*, wrote *The Tech-Wise Family* to help Christians "find the proper place for technology in our family lives—and how to keep it there."[40] Crouch's explanation of the "proper place" helps us understand that technology does have a place and that we do well to know where that is and where it isn't. We won't flourish if we ignore the good gifts which God gives us in technology. Nor will we flourish if we assume that the presence of one good gift in technology means that every function of technology is itself a good gift.

Flourishing is a result of applying wisdom. Crouch warns, "The pace of technological change has surpassed anyone's capacity to develop enough wisdom to handle it."[41] Advertisers promise the best digital devices are those that can get you the most information the fastest. They say that you need the new. Biblical wisdom explains that true flourishing comes as we wisely apply the brakes.

---

40 Andy Crouch, *The Tech-Wise Family: Everyday Steps for Putting Technology in Its Proper Place* (Grand Rapids: Baker Academic, 2017), p. 16.

41 Crouch, *The Tech-Wise Family*, p. 17.

Crouch continues,

> *Technology is in its proper place when it helps us bond with the real people we have been given to love . . . when it starts great conversations . . . when it helps us take care of the fragile bodies we inhabit . . . when it helps us acquire skill and mastery of domains that are the glory of human culture . . . when it helps us cultivate awe for the created world we are part of and responsible for stewarding . . . only when we use it with intention and care.*[42]

Human flourishing in a digital age demands that we not only find the proper place of technology and digital devices, but that we labor to continually reexamine that place and adjust as necessary. Indeed, with each new upgrade and app we will need to rethink technology's proper place.

Do I Know When to Unplug?

There is one final subcategory that we need to address in the issue of flourishing. While we

---

42 Crouch, *The Tech-Wise Family*, pp. 20–21.

have undoubtedly left a number of important topics or themes untouched, we would be negligent not to discuss the art of unplugging. So, do you know when to unplug? And do you know how?

Tony Reinke writes,

> *Faced with the world's endless buffet of digital spectacles, Christians will choose to seasonally step away, to power down the screens around them, for a day or a week or a couple of weeks. We will choose to fast from the spectacle industry, to digitally detox as a way to remind ourselves that we live in this age of spectacles as foreigners.*[43]

Smothered seeds don't flourish. Nor do Christians who fail to unplug.

Practicing Digital Sabbath

Author Pete Scazzero defines Sabbath as "a twenty-four-hour block of time in which we stop work, enjoy rest, practice delight, and contemplate

---

43 Tony Reinke, *Competing Spectacles: Treasuring Christ in the Media Age* (Wheaton: Crossway, 2019), pp. 134–135.

God."[44] Digital users will stop digital work, enjoy uninterrupted rest, practice deep delight, and contemplate God who is above and beyond any digital realm. This intentional habit provides a formational effect on us as we disconnect from our digital mediums and live. Scazzero explains, "Through any and every means possible, on Sabbath we seek to feast on the miracle of life with our senses."[45] In doing so, we exchange our disembodied experiences through a digital medium for embodied enjoyment with our own senses.

Digital Sabbaths require digitally disconnecting. For smartphone users, seasonal digital monkery will doubtless become an essential discipline for healthy Christian living.[46] Put the phone in a room other than the one in which you sleep and use an alarm clock. Leave the work phone in a non-distracting location while you are at home. Create a screen-free room or space in your house. Practice "no-screen"

---

44 Peter Scazzero, *The Emotionally Healthy Leader: How Transforming Your Inner Life Will Deeply Transform Your Church, Team and the World* (Grand Rapids: Zondervan, 2015), p. 144.

45 Scazzero, *The Emotionally Healthy Leader*, p. 148.

46 Reinke, *12 Ways Your Phone Is Changing You*, p. 196.

days. Consider abandoning your smartphone altogether. God has commanded his people to use one day a week to forsake other distractions in order to delight in him.

The Biblical Basis for Digital Sabbath

Having rescued his people from Pharaoh's oppressive hand (under which Israel experienced the opposite of flourishing), God gave them the Ten Commandments. These commandments were to serve as guardrails for people plagued by sin in a world also plagued by sin. Walter Chantry, in his book *Call the Sabbath a Delight*, writes, "The Ten Commandments ... are the Lord's summary of moral law, his definition of loving behavior."[47] God's commandments are never burdensome (1 John 5:3); they put us on the path to flourishing.

God's fourth commandment, for Sabbath rest, is particularly important for our discussion on what it means to flourish in a digital age. In this commandment, Moses records,

47 Walter Chantry, *Call the Sabbath a Delight* (Edinburgh: Banner of Truth, 1991), p. 17.

> *Remember the Sabbath day, to keep it holy. Six days you shall labor, and do all your work, but the seventh day is a Sabbath to the* Lord *your God. On it you shall not do any work, you, or your son, or your daughter, your male servant, or your female servant, or your livestock, or the sojourner who is within your gates. For in six days the* Lord *made heaven and earth, the sea, and all that is in them, and rested on the seventh day. Therefore the* Lord *blessed the Sabbath day and made it holy (Ex. 20:8–11).*

Chantry explains, "The Sabbath was made for man's welfare. It was always designed for man's good."[48] God gave us the Sabbath that we would flourish. He has commanded a pattern of rest and renewal.

The prophet Isaiah also highlights the flourishing effect of honoring the Sabbath:

> *If you turn back your foot from the Sabbath,*
> *from doing your pleasure on my holy day,*
> *and call the Sabbath a delight*
> *and the holy day of the* Lord *honorable;*

---

48 Chantry, *Call the Sabbath a Delight*, p. 50.

if you honor it, not going your own ways,
or seeking your own pleasure, or
talking idly;
then you shall take delight in the LORD,
and I will make you ride on the heights
of the earth;
I will feed you with the heritage of Jacob
your father,
for the mouth of the LORD has spoken.
(Is. 58:13–14)

The promises of God are astounding here. He promises that we will "delight in the LORD" and that we will "ride on the heights of the earth" and that he himself will feed us "with the heritage of Jacob your father" (v. 14). While it is beyond the scope of this book to explain in full the details of these promises, let it suffice to say that God is promising his people a flourishing life. This flourishing was theirs through the gift of the Sabbath.

Christian, those promises are yours in Christ. In fact, the blessings in Christ are richer and deeper and more wonderful than even those promises can contain. So, unplug and enjoy them. They cannot be mediated through any digital device. They must be embraced by faith.

Am I Flourishing or Withering?

There is a zombie-like effect to those who spend too much time on devices. When they finally emerge from their digital world, it's as though they have to rediscover analog life. The sun hurts their eyes. The quiet frightens them. This is a picture of withering. In contrast, there is a budding joy in the eyes of a woman who is able to video chat with her elderly father states away. He is able to hear his favorite hymns sung by his daughter. She can send pictures of his great-grandchildren to the digital picture frame that sits beside his chair. The pictures automatically upload and display while he eats another dinner alone. Technology helps him to flourish.

God's vision for human flourishing is one in which we live with an awareness of the shaping influence of our technologies. We exercise dominion over those technologies by remembering our Godward direction and holding to biblical wisdom in our usage. So, are you a better person as a result of owning a phone or having a social media account? Does the last app you downloaded encourage you to flourish and thrive? Everything shapes us somehow. God calls you to mindfully engage with digital devices as an act of obediently exercising dominion and pursuing his vision for your flourishing.

Discussion Questions

1. How would you describe a biblical portrait of human flourishing?
2. In what ways has Satan used digital devices in his opposition to God's goal of human flourishing?
3. How does the call to be holy influence your use of digital devices?
4. Have you ever felt yourself withering as a result of your digital devices? Describe that experience.
5. What would a digital sabbath look like in your life?

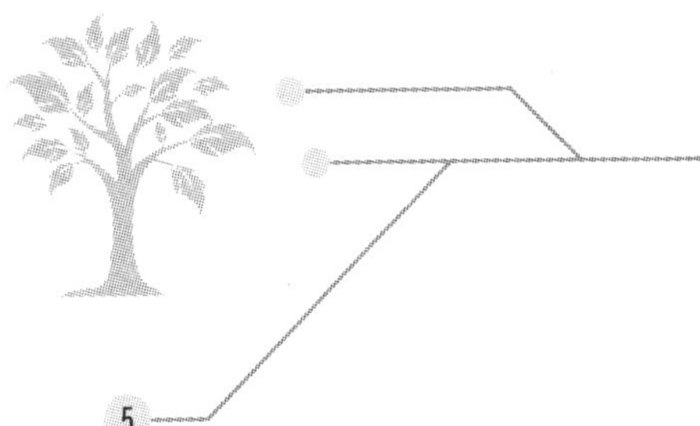

Can I Discern Wisdom and Folly?

It's hard to be tech-wise, because it's hard to be wise.

Amy Crouch[49]

Biblical authors contrast the wise and the foolish. They warn us of the perils of the fool. Solomon articulates what Wisdom personified would say to the fool who refused her warning:

49 Amy Crouch and Andy Crouch. *My Tech-Wise Life: Growing Up and Making Choices in a World of Devices* (Grand Rapids: Baker, 2020), p. 16.

Because I have called and you refused to listen,
have stretched out my hand and no one has heeded,
because you have ignored all my counsel
and would have none of my reproof,
I also will laugh at your calamity;
I will mock when terror strikes you,
when terror strikes you like a storm
and your calamity comes like a whirlwind,
when distress and anguish come upon you.
(Prov. 1:24–27)

It is not hard to imagine the digital outworking of such foolishness. Derek Kidner explains that the biblical fool, "is the kind of person who is easily led, gullible, silly. Mentally he is naïve . . . morally he is willful and irresponsible. . . . The simple . . . is no halfwit; he is a person whose instability could be rectified, but who prefers not to accept discipline in the school of wisdom."[50] You probably know some digital fools.

In contrast, the biblical authors honor and celebrate the wise man. Solomon writes, "The

---

50 Derek Kidner, *Proverbs*, Tyndale Old Testament Commentary (Downers Grove: Intervarsity, 2009), pp. 36–37.

wise will inherit honor" (Prov. 3:35). Jesus points us to the wise man who built his house on the rock instead of building on the sand (Matt. 7:24–27). I hope you know some people who are wise. Even more so, I hope that you seek and apply wisdom.

Seek Wisdom as You Examine Digital Practices

Christians seek wisdom as we examine our existing digital practices. Familiarity breeds assumptions and, familiar with the digital world, we assume that our digital habits are normal. We assume they are healthy. Neil Postman warns us, "There is no more disturbing consequence of the electronic and graphic revolution than this: that the world as given to us through television seems natural, not bizarre."[51] We are not shocked. But we should be.

When was the last time you stepped away from your digital devices to examine how you use them? Perhaps never. Here are some diagnostic questions to help examine your digital practices:

- How many digital devices do you own?

51 Postman, *Entertaining Ourselves to Death*, p. 79.

- How quickly do you use a digital device after waking up?
- To which device do you give the most time or attention?
- How often do you check your digital devices?
- Do you limit when you get notifications?
- How close is your phone to you right now?
- When is the last time you had device-free time with another person?
- When is the last time you went twenty-four hours without a digital device?

King Solomon writes, "I turned my heart to know and to search out and to seek wisdom and the scheme of things, and to know the wickedness of folly and the foolishness that is madness" (Ecc. 7:25). Christian, is that you? Have you turned your heart to know and search out and seek wisdom and the scheme of digital things? The apostle Paul urges you to seek wisdom and not remain ignorant of Satan's designs (2

Cor. 2:11). Beware of the folly of the world and the schemes of the devil as you exercise control over your digital devices.

Exercising dominion over digital content requires intentionality and awareness. It requires wisdom. Users who do not examine their current digital practices continue to float in the direction determined by the digital world, the end of which is folly.

Beware the Digital Fool

Not all of our digital habits and liturgies are good. Throughout the book of Proverbs, Solomon warns us through the character known as "the fool." Fools mindlessly consume media and adopt technological advances without discernment. Derek Kidner offers this description of the fool:

> *The root of his trouble is spiritual, not mental. He likes his folly, going back to it 'like a dog that returns to his vomit' (26:11); he has no reverence for truth, preferring comfortable illusions.... At bottom, what he is rejecting is the fear of the Lord (1:29): it is this that constitutes him a fool, and this makes his*

> *complacency tragic; for 'the careless ease of fools shall destroy them' (1:32).*[52]

A digital fool loves his digital destruction. He returns to it night after night, knowing his binge-watching causes him to sleep through the alarm and miss another shift at work. He dismisses the warnings of friends and family, instead heeding the beckoning notifications buzzing and flashing from his phone. He covers up the pain of loneliness with another game or another tweet while he sits alone in a room that used to be filled with friends. In the dazed reflection of his device he begins to think, "I don't really need a life outside of my digital life. I don't really need a family outside of this rectangle in my hands. I have everything I need. There is nothing more." Yes, "The fool says in his heart, 'There is no God.'" (Ps. 14:1).

Create a New Liturgy

Our habits and liturgies shape us, and we've seen the increasing impact of digital habits and liturgies. Therefore, wisdom calls us to create

---

52 Kidner, *Proverbs*, p. 40.

a new liturgy that maximizes the benefits of digital connectedness while keeping its dangers in check. This new liturgy will help us to pursue God's vision of human flourishing in a digital age. What we need are new life disciplines birthed from a new set of life priorities and empowered by our new-life freedom in Jesus Christ.[53]

If we are removing a habit that has taken much of our time and shaped many of our experiences and emotions, we must fill the void. But with what? Some people may pick up a hand-driven habit such as handwriting cards of encouragement to friends and family. We can replace our numerous text-message conversations with one undistracted coffee date with a friend. We can pick up a paperback copy of a book or magazine. We can take a walk on the local nature trail, without feeling the need to post a picture on social media or worry about counting steps. We can replace mindlessly scrolling through posts with mindfully meditating on a passage of Scripture. We can pray. John Piper points out, "One of the great

---

53 Reinke, *12 Ways Your Phone Is Changing You*, p. 21.

uses of Twitter and Facebook will be to prove at the Last Day that prayerlessness was not from lack of time."[54]

Prayer, the Word, and even our participation in the local church can be improved by disconnecting digitally. Tony Reinke suggests,

> *Maybe this is a key function of church attendance in the digital age. We must withdraw from our online worlds to gather as a body in our local churches. We gather to be seen, to feel awkward, and perhaps to feel a little unheard and underappreciated, all on purpose. In obedience to the biblical command to not forsake meeting together, we each come as one small piece, one individual member, one body part, in order to find purpose, life, and value in union with the rest of the living body of Christ.*[55]

As the church gathers, we look one another in the eye, rejoicing and weeping together. We sing next to each other, both in tune and out of

---

54 John Piper, Twitter post, @JohnPiper, October 20, 2009, 6:02 p.m.; https://twitter.com/johnpiper/status/5027319857/

55 Reinke, *12 Ways Your Phone Is Changing You*, p. 72.

tune. We taste the bread and wine of the Lord's Supper. We hear the tremor in the praying man's voice. We shake our brother's or sister's hand in greeting. Digital devices fail us by not delivering many of life's greatest joys. New liturgies, in which we better exercise dominion over our devices, will help us rediscover these joys.

A Few More Wisdom Practices

As you seek to apply wisdom to your digital practices, you will have to determine your own habits and liturgies. Examine the wisdom and folly of your habits and adjust accordingly. Here is a list of possible starting points:

1. *Charge your phone in a different room while you sleep.* Go back to the old-school alarm clock. I'm sure they are still for sale at a local drug store or online. This will eliminate the possibility of reaching over to check the time only to get lost in a maze of "What Harry Potter character are you?" at 3:00 a.m. Pay attention to how this change affects your sleep and your overall mental attitude.

2. *Set priorities for your morning that you will accomplish before using your phone.* Decide the pace of your day with activities that you choose (coffee, Bible study, a good book) rather than being forced into a responsive mode by checking email or social media. Make a list of five to ten activities to which you want to give priority over digital engagement. Or, if your schedule is regular enough, set a time range in which you will not check your phone.

3. *Develop guidelines for your digital usage during the day.* How much time on a digital device is too much for you? Two hours? Four hours? Eight hours? The chances are that you have no idea how much time you actually spend on digital devices. Various apps can be helpful tools for measuring this in your home. The Screen Time function of iPhones will also inform you of battery usage and screen time usage, including how much time the screen has been on and a breakdown of apps used. Then use a similar app or function to

set an appropriate limit to your digital usage. This is a matter of you exercising dominion over your devices rather than being mindlessly consumed by them.

4. *Put your phone away during meals.* Don't put it face down on the table. Put it away. In another room. Out of sight (and earshot). Enjoy the meal with whomever is there and foster conversation. If needed, here are some discussion questions: What was the best part of your day? What was the hardest part of your day? If you could have dinner with five people (dead or alive), who would you choose? What is one thing that you think you did well today?
5. *Regularly thank God for the blessing of technology.* When is the last time you thanked God for technology? If it's been a while, perhaps too little of your digital usage is pointing you in a Godward direction. Use technology for Godward purposes such as talking with missionaries or listening to encouraging podcasts. And then thank God for that technology. Just

this week I received a picture of a church member who is visiting one of our missionaries overseas. What a gift the Lord has given us in technology!

6. *Set a bedtime for digital devices*. Choose that time and stick to it. Allow your mind to calm down and release the digital distractions of the day. Put your devices to sleep so that you can put yourself to rest.

7. *Practice regular digital-free days or seasons of fasting*. This may be a weekly Sabbath practice during which you disconnect and focus on the Lord through your senses. You may consider a longer season of digital fasting.

8. *Identify certain events that you can better enjoy without your phone*. You don't need your phone for everything, and some events will be better experienced without your phone at all. Think about leaving your phone in the car when you go to church on Sunday morning. Focus on greeting the people around you. Your phone won't grow legs and walk away.

Yes, something could possibly happen in which someone needs to get in touch with you. However, in all of the Sundays that you've attended church, how many of those emergencies have occurred during that one hour? If you'd feel better keeping your phone with you, take it in, but commit to putting it face down under your chair or in your purse until the service is over.

9. *Commit to one face-to-face meeting per week that is phone-free*. Perhaps you and a friend could commit to meeting and discussing how your digital habits have gone over the past week.
10. *Ask your kids to describe your digital habits*. Then repent. No more needs saying here. Ouch!

There are many other ways you can apply biblical wisdom to your digital habits. Get together with a friend to talk through this list and discuss what you would add.

We don't drift toward wisdom. And our digital devices don't naturally lead us toward wisdom.

The sinful direction of our hearts produces the foolish use of our devices. We are sinners and we are fools. But God has given us good wisdom by which to live. As you seek to exercise digital dominion and take control of your devices, regularly ask, "Can I discern wisdom and folly?"

Discussion Questions

1. Describe some marks of wisdom in using digital devices. Describe some marks of folly.
2. How does being wise with digital devices bring honor and glory to God?
3. What is one way that you have been foolish with digital devices? How has that folly impacted you and those around you?
4. If you could help your friends and family develop a wise practice in the way they handle digital devices, which one would you choose and why?

5. Which of the wisdom practices presented in this chapter do you most need to apply?

Am I Being Missional?

What would be involved in a missionary encounter between the gospel and this whole way of perceiving, thinking, and living that we call "digital culture?"

Lesslie Newbigin, paraphrased[56]

Imagine telling your spouse, "Honey, I was faithful to you in every aspect of my life . . . except

56 Newbigin actually poses the question, "What would be involved in a missionary encounter between the gospel and this whole way of perceiving, thinking, and living that we call 'modern Western culture'?" Lesslie Newbigin, *Foolishness to the Greeks*, p. 1.

with my digital devices, where I pretended like you didn't exist." Unfortunately, that's essentially what many Christians have said to Jesus. We honor him in many areas of our lives, but with our digital devices we've sidestepped his lordship and completely ignored his command to make disciples. Almost faithful is unfaithful.

The apostle Paul wanted to get the gospel to everyone. Paul quoted Isaiah as he spurred believers in Rome to leverage their lives for the gospel: "How beautiful are the feet of those who preach the good news?" (Rom. 10:15; cf. Is. 52:7). Believer, how beautiful is your digital footprint? While job applicants wonder what impact their digital footprint will have on their chances of being hired, believers should consider their digital footprint as a reflection of the reputation of Jesus.

Have you ever thought through your role as a digital missionary? As you scroll through your feed, have you considered offering the hope of the gospel? Have you considered recording your testimony and posting it to your platforms? Is the gospel the answer to Facebook's prompting question, "What's on your mind...?" or to Twitter's prompt, "What's happening?"

You can either mindlessly scroll or missionally engage. But you can't do both. Not at the same time. So, resolve to approach the digital world with a missionary mindset, with gospel intentionality. Before we consider how to do that, let's first clarify our mission.

Clarifying the Mission and Missions

As noted in chapter one, God created humanity to bear his image and fill the world with others who would bear his image. Thus our mission is to reflect the character of God to the world and to see others come to reflect him through Christ.

The resurrected Jesus said to his disciples,

> *All authority in heaven and on earth has been given to me. Go therefore and make disciples of all nations, baptizing them in the name of the Father and of the Son and of the Holy Spirit, teaching them to observe all that I have commanded you. And behold, I am with you always, to the end of the age (Matt. 28:18–20).*

Known as "The Great Commission," Jesus' words to his disciples in Matthew 28 are intended for you. Yes, you are called to make disciples of all nations. You are called to this great mission.

You can pursue many causes with your life. You can feed the hungry in the slums of India. You can provide disaster relief in the mountains of South America. And while Christians may be found doing these and other important efforts, our mission as Christians is this: to make disciples of Jesus Christ. This is our singular purpose in life, and in death. David Mathis offers this pointed explanation: "The goal of missions is the worldwide worship of the God-man by his redeemed people from every tribe, tongue, and nation. The outcome of missions is all peoples delighting to praise Jesus. And the motivation for missions is the enjoyment that his people have in him. Missions aims at, brings about, and is fueled by the worship of Jesus."[57] Having been gripped by the glory of Jesus through our own salvation, we lay down our lives for the glory of Jesus in the salvation of others. Your worship of Jesus ought to have implications for your digital platforms. You are meant to be a digital missionary.

---

57 John Piper and David Mathis, *Finish the Mission: Bring the Gospel to the Unreached and Unengaged* (Wheaton: Crossway, 2012), p. 14.

Many Christians have grown up thinking that they needed to get onto an airplane to do missions. Missiologist Michael Goheen writes, "What defines missions today is not exclusively the crossing of cultural or national boundaries with the gospel but creating a gospel witness where it is absent or weak."[58] You don't have to look very far to conclude that the gospel witness online is absent or weak.

Have you considered how Jesus' command to "make disciples of all nations" (Matt. 28:19) applies to your use of digital devices? As long as you remain ignorant of these implications, you are not exercising digital dominion—not for God's purposes. You have lost control if your digital practices are not producing obedience to King Jesus. So, bring your digital devices under control for Great Commission purposes.

Shifting from Mindlessly Scrolling to Missionally Engaging

Your digital devices can become powerful tools in a digital mission field. Jesus' words to you to "make disciples of all nations" (Matt. 28:19)

---

58 Michael Goheen, *Introducing Christian Mission Today: Scripture, History and Issues* (Downers Grove: IVP Academic, 2014), p. 403.

ought to fuel your digital engagement. His mission deserves our active obedience not our passive consideration.

But how can you move from mindlessly scrolling to missionally engaging? Let's recognize that Christians will approach a digital mission field with different tactics, and that's okay. Some are more comfortable engaging a digital world than others. Christians should be comfortable with their own convictions regarding digital devices. However, here are some principles that can help you make the shift from mindlessly scrolling to missionally engaging.

Pray

Prayer is non-negotiable in the Christian life. Paul left no room for doubt as he wrote to the Thessalonians, "pray without ceasing" (1 Thes. 5:17). There is nothing—including digital activity—that should be done without prayer.

Paul also highlighted the place of prayer in evangelism, requesting prayer for gospel effectiveness (Col. 4:3; 2 Thes. 3:1). Paul knew he couldn't advance the gospel without the prayers of other believers. And he knew their prayers were effective. He wrote to the Philippians,

> *. . . for I know that through your prayers and the help of the Spirit of Jesus Christ this will turn out for my deliverance, as it is my eager expectation and hope that I will not be at all ashamed, but that with full courage now as always Christ will be honored in my body, whether by life or by death (Phil. 1:19–20).*

Paul recognized the importance of prayer as he sought the glory of Christ in his life. Do you?

If you are going to engage the digital world like a missionary, lay a foundation of prayer. Imagine a missionary who didn't pray or ask for prayer. It sounds ridiculous, doesn't it? Well, it is. And it is equally ridiculous for you to think that you can successfully engage the digital world for Christ without prayer.

Post like a missionary

Have you ever seen a fellow Christian post something and thought, "Why in the world would they post that?!" I have! I've wondered how people could post with such little regard for others. I've seen racially insensitive posts from believers, posts that were demeaning of others, and forms of posts I found curious. I'm usually not close enough to these people to have an in-person conversation, so I just scroll past without comment. In the few instances in which I've had conversations with them, I've found that they used the phrase "Oh, I didn't think. . . ." Yep, there's the problem. They didn't think.

Christian, think like a missionary. When you open up your digital device, think like a missionary. Perhaps Christians would do well to make their log-in password "I am a missionary." (That's not my password, by the way!)

If you are going to make the shift from mindlessly scrolling to missionally engaging the digital world, think and post like a missionary. This probably means that you're going to have to forgo posting that political article that crushes the other side. You can't missionally engage someone while belittling them.

Do the work of evangelism

If the digital world is a mission field, do the work of evangelism. This means that you will need to begin to identify the idols that are displayed online. We'll talk about how Paul did that in the next section. But it also means that you can leverage your posts for evangelistic purposes.

Jesus regularly invited people to himself: "Come to me, all who labor and are heavy laden, and I will give you rest" (Matt. 11:28). "I am the bread of life; whoever comes to me shall not hunger, and whoever believes in me shall never thirst" (John 6:35). He calls people, even compels them, to come to him and place their trust in him. The question that confronts his followers is: Do we? He left us no room for doubt as he said, "Follow me, and I will make you fishers of men" (Matt. 4:19). He explained, "The harvest is plentiful, but the laborers are few" (Luke 10:2). The harvest is plentiful in your digital platform. Do the work of evangelism.

Do the work of follow-up

Digital platforms are not good places for conversations. Sure, you can get into an argument online. But it's hard, if it's even possible, to have a reasoned conversation there.

If you are going to make the shift from mindless consumption to active and missional participation, you may need to make a mental shift here. Don't expect to have complete conversations on digital platforms. Begin thinking of online engagements as the first conversation that will hopefully lead to an in-person follow-up.

Then do the work of follow-up. When you see online a friend like or comment on your spiritually oriented post, send them a direct message and ask if you can connect offline.

Go on mission in community

One of the most dangerous mistakes we can make online is to think that we are all alone. Digital platforms give us a false sense of isolation and anonymity. But God has placed Christians in community in the local church.

Christian, allow your local church to have a voice in your online engagement. Give church members the authority to point out any of your online activity that may be unwise. But correction is not the only piece of community. Recruit them to be your team in digital missions.

If you are going to make the shift from mindlessly scrolling to missionally engaging, invite the church. Rally together with some other believers and let them know about your desire to be an online missionary. Begin to encourage each other and pray for each other. Don't go at it alone. Go on mission in community.

Engaging a Digital Areopagus

The apostle Paul modeled the missionary life. But how would Paul navigate a digital landscape? How would he communicate the gospel to digital natives?

Among Paul's many missionary interactions, his intentional engagement at the Areopagus in Athens has been the source of study for many hopeful missionaries. Perhaps this account has something to offer to Christians as they seek to engage online neighbors and nations with the gospel.

Here are five lessons we can learn from Paul's experience at the Areopagus:

Take note when your spirit is provoked within you

As the apostle Paul waited at Athens, "his spirit was provoked within him as he saw that the city was full of idols" (Acts 17:16). Based on what he saw, Paul began his plea: "Men of Athens, I perceive that in every way you are very religious" (Acts 17:22). His spirit was provoked and his mouth was moved to preach.

Christian, as you navigate the digital world, your spirit will be provoked. Take note. You ought to be bothered by the idolatry on display. This is the missionary burden. If you are not provoked, beware. You have grown comfortable and familiar with enemy territory.

How comfortable are you scrolling past the idolatrous posts of your neighbors and friends? Does it bother you? Does it prompt you to prayer?

When it comes to engaging a digital Areopagus with the gospel, a missionary mentality will include a heartbreaking burden. Each picture is both a display of what they value and a plea for approval and applause. On the other side of that post, no matter how ugly, is a person who needs the gospel. Beware a calloused heart where there should be a provoked spirit.

Know that idolatry is expressed culturally in shared spaces

Paul saw that the city was full of idols. He wasn't primarily bothered by the physical carvings, but by those men and women made in the image of God—and made to know the One True God—who would worship these idols. Commentator John Stott notes,

> *First and foremost, what [Paul] saw was neither the beauty nor the brilliance of the city, but its idolatry. The adjective Luke uses (kateidolos) occurs nowhere else in the New Testament and has not been found in any other Greek literature. Although most English versions render it 'full of idols', the idea conveyed seems to be that the city was 'under' them. We might say that it was 'smothered with idols' or 'swamped' by them.*[59]

The physical landscape of the Areopagus revealed the religious nature of the Athenians. Similarly, the digital landscape of our social media accounts reveals the religious nature of our hearts. If the human heart is an idol factory, the internet is an Areopagus. There our idols are on full display.

This means that when we critique an article posted by someone online, we need to remember that we are confronting their idols. They will likely respond with the sensitivity and emotion of someone whose object of worship

---

59 John Stott, *The Message of Acts*, The Bible Speaks Today (Downers Grove: Intervarsity, 1991), p. 277.

has just been criticized. Don't be surprised when the comment you thought was harmless is taken with great offense.

Let's clarify something here. You may be burdened or disturbed by something because it doesn't fit your view of the world and the way things should be. However, there is a difference between that and what Paul felt, which was a heartbreak that the Athenians were missing God. R. Kent Hughes explains that Paul "was angry about a lie. As a Jewish monotheist, he would have been disturbed. As a Christian apostle, he was even more enraged! Every idol demonstrated the Athenians' hunger for God, but it also testified to their spiritual emptiness. Ignorant of the one true God, the Athenians were lost!"[60] A lot of Christians are provoked by things that bother them, but you could essentially remove God from their disagreement and not much would change. They're more provoked by a breach of their moral preferences than by the profaning of God's name.

---

60 R. Kent Hughes, *Acts: The Church Afire*, Preaching the Word (Wheaton: Crossway, 1996), p. 230.

Some of us aren't even provoked. We don't feel anything. Apathy has taken root. We're not burdened by idolatry because we don't deeply love true worship of the One True God.

As you scroll through your social media feed or your digital news source, the idolatry of your friends and your world passes before your eyes. It's easy to scroll when we forget that we are looking at idols.

Remember the difference between reasoning and reacting

Luke records that Paul, "reasoned in the synagogue with the Jews and the devout persons, and in the marketplace every day with those who happened to be there. Some of the Epicurean and Stoic philosophers also conversed with him" (Acts 17:17–18). The result of this interaction was favorable. It led to more conversation. Luke continues, "And they took him and brought him to the Areopagus, saying, 'May we know what this new teaching is that you are presenting? For you bring some strange things to our ears. We wish to know therefore what these things mean'" (Acts 17:19–20).

Paul reasoned. There is a difference between reasoning and reacting as it's commonly practiced online today. Digital reaction leads to quick comments and unnecessarily polarizing posts. We see the headline and we react. Paul, on the other hand, saw the idols and reasoned.

If you approached the internet with the heart, and self-control, of a missionary, would you react the way you currently do? Would a missionary mindset cause you to walk away before you hit the next keystroke?

It is near impossible to reason thoroughly in a quotable tweet. Divisive reactions require few words. But the missionary task calls us to reasoning not just reacting.

Preach Jesus and the resurrection

Luke also recounts, "And some said, 'What does this babbler wish to say?' Others said, 'He seems to be a preacher of foreign divinities'—because he was preaching Jesus and the resurrection" (Acts 17:18).

No matter where Paul's missionary journeys took him, his message remained the same: Christ crucified and resurrected. This remained his constant theme and song.

Christian, preach Jesus and the resurrection in the digital world. More than you post political articles or opinion pieces, preach Jesus. Preach him so often that others in your digital sphere of influence begin to say, "He seems to be a promoter of foreign divinities. He doesn't post like us."

As Paul engaged the worshippers of unknown divinities in the Areopagus, he preached Jesus. As you engage digital worshippers, preach Jesus. That friend that posts one-sided political monologues has developed a reputation based on those opinionated posts. Believer, make yourself known as one who preaches Jesus.

Accept that you will experience both opposition and open doors, and that God can use both

Luke concludes his account, "Now when they heard of the resurrection of the dead, some mocked. But others said, 'We will hear you again about this.' So Paul went out from their midst. But some men joined him and believed, among whom also were Dionysius the Areopagite and a woman named Damaris and others with them" (Acts 17:32–34).

Christian, if you resolve to preach Jesus in a digital Areopagus, you will experience opposition. There will be some, perhaps many, that mock you and ridicule you. They will dismiss you as foolish or arrogant or both.

But there will also be some who say, "We will hear you again about this." A missionary approach that takes the gospel to the digital world will bear fruit. The Word will not return void.

And know that God will use both the opposition and the open doors to advance his gospel. It may advance through your digital dismissal as it advanced through Paul's imprisonment (Phil. 1:12). Or it may advance as some respond favorably. Either way, as Paul the missionary did, we rejoice.

Don't Collect Digital Seashells

On May 20, 2000, pastor John Piper pleaded with 40,000 college students not to waste their lives. Piper offered this illustration to the crowd as he read from *Reader's Digest*: "Bob and Penny took . . . early retirement from their jobs in the Northeast five years ago when he was 59 and she was 51. Now they live in Punta Gorda, Florida, where they cruise on their 30-foot trawler, play softball, and collect shells." He then warned them, "The American Dream:

come to the end of your life—*your one and only life*—and let the last great work before you give an account to your Creator be, 'I collected shells. See my shells.'"[61]

That sermon resonated with college students in their late teenage years and early twenties. Many of them were propelled onto the mission field. But I fear that twenty years later some of those students—now in their late thirties or early forties—are clicking "next episode" as they collect digital seashells.

Don't waste your life collecting digital seashells. You have one life to make much of Christ. And in his providence, God positioned you in a moment in time when you have the ability to reach the nations with the gospel. You can leverage a small device in your pocket for the greatest mission in the history of the world. Do you see the opportunity in front of you?! How many missionaries throughout church history would have wept tears of joy if they had been given the digital device that you have on your

---

61 John Piper, "Boasting Only in the Cross," sermon delivered May 20, 2000 in Memphis, Tennessee at Passion's OneDay 2000; https://www.desiringgod.org/messages/boasting-only-in-the-cross. Quoted in J.D. Greear's *What Are You Going to Do with Your Life?* (Nashville, TN: Lifeway Christian Resources, 2020).

table? They laid down their lives for the mission; surely you can leverage your device.

Meditate on the glory of Jesus Christ. Stand in awe of the salvation that you enjoy because of his perfect life and sacrificial death. Rejoice that he delights to use imperfect vessels to spread the good news of his salvation to others. And then, with a face that is radiant as you've beheld his goodness, pick up your digital device and use it to make much of Jesus Christ.

Discussion Questions

1. How would you describe the Great Commission? How should it impact Christians today?
2. Which of the principles in "Shifting from Mindlessly Scrolling to Missionally Engaging" do you need to apply?
3. Describe one person that uses their digital devices for missional purposes.
4. As you read about Paul's approach to the Areopagus in Acts 17, which principle most applied to your digital

life? What can you do differently as you take a missional approach to your digital devices?

5. How would you like to see God use your digital activity for his glory? If you began to pray that way, what might that prayer include?

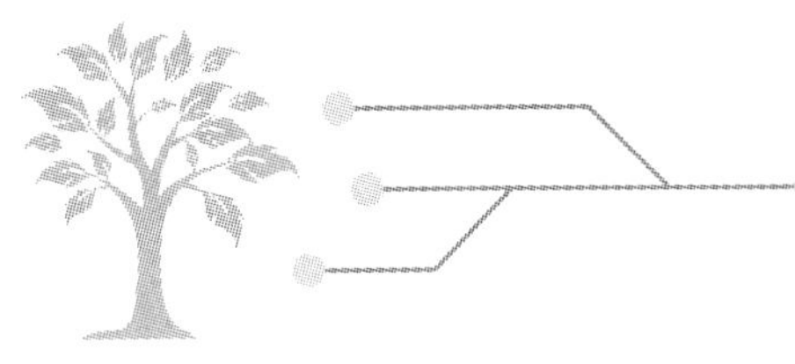

Conclusion

Wise Christians tread carefully in digital waters. Yet we embrace the digital revolution as an opportunity to advance the gospel. Technology provides new and improved communication platforms on which Christians boldly herald the good news of Christ crucified. God sovereignly orchestrates the creation of media platforms for his renown. Our hearts are not left to their own devices, but are encouraged by the reviving effects of God's Word. God is at work both in us and through us for such a time as this. The digital revolution is a moment in the divine timeline.

Biblical wisdom exposes the shaping influence of our habits and liturgies, whether we live in the Stone Age or the Digital Age. Our tools mold us even as we use them. Christians seize the opportunities provided in this age and work to remember their Godward direction. They exercise dominion over their digital devices, all to the glory of God.

My prayer throughout this book is that you would exercise dominion in your digital world. Some readers will walk away convinced that they need to use their devices less and others that they need to use their devices more. Either way, I hope you move forward on purpose. I hope that at the end of your day you feel the joy of God-honoring productivity more often than the shame of uncontrolled posting. Above all, I hope that when your eyes turn to a digital screen, they will be governed by a heart that is captivated by the glory of Christ.

Dedicated to Lauren, Aiden, and Carter.
I love you more than any digital device.
And I pray that you can leverage your
devices well.